To my nephew, ANDREW CARR WOOD, of the Chesapeake Bay Foundation,
who works to save the wetlands of my childhood.

ACKNOWLEDGMENTS:
I would like to thank Dr. Julie Mankiewicz and her AP Environmental Science students at Bronx High School of Science:
Andrea Alfano, Ankush Chadha, Sean Harpal, Siri Mclean, Eliza Phillips, Danny Tai, and Connie Yan—for helping me
to verify the facts in this book, and for being such careful maze-solvers!

Library of Congress Cataloging-in-Publication Data

Munro, Roxie.
 Ecomazes : twelve Earth adventures / by Roxie Munro.
   p. cm.
 ISBN 978-1-4027-6393-9
 1. Ecological regions--Juvenile literature. 2. Biotic communities--
Juvenile literature. 3. Maze puzzles. I. Title.
 QH541.14.M86 2010
 577--dc22   2009029102

Lot #:10 9 8 7 6 5 4 3 2
05/10
Published by Sterling Publishing Co., Inc.
387 Park Avenue South, New York, NY 10016
Text and illustrations © 2010 by Roxie Munro
Distributed in Canada by Sterling Publishing
c/o Canadian Manda Group, 165 Dufferin Street
Toronto, Ontario, Canada M6K 3H6
Distributed in the United Kingdom by GMC Distribution Services
Castle Place, 166 High Street, Lewes, East Sussex, England BN7 1XU
Distributed in Australia by Capricorn Link (Australia) Pty. Ltd.
P.O. Box 704, Windsor, NSW 2756, Australia

Sterling ISBN 978-1-4027-6393-9

For information about custom editions, special sales, premium and
corporate purchases, please contact Sterling Special Sales
Department at 800-805-5489 or specialsales@sterlingpublishing.com.

Designed by Kate Moll
The artwork for this book was prepared using black and
colored inks on Strathmore paper.

EcoMazes

TWELVE EARTH ADVENTURES

by
ROXIE MUNRO

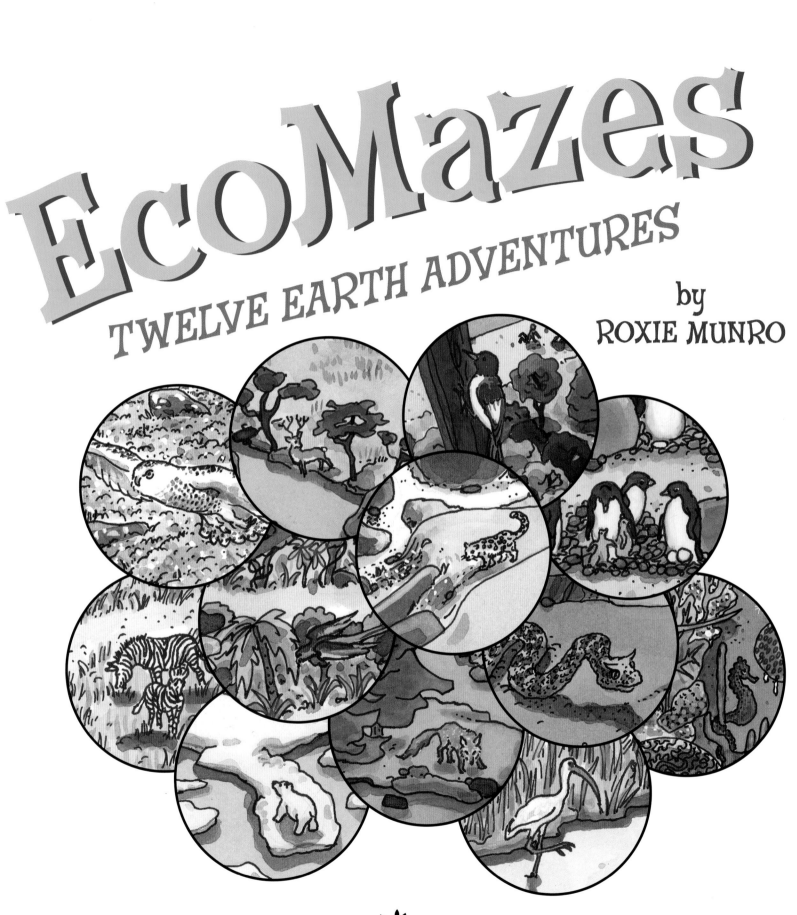

STERLING

New York / London
www.sterlingpublishing.com/kids

Look for more info—as well as the solutions to each maze—at the back of this book.

Wherever on Earth you find yourself, YOU are part of an ecosystem!

Walking alone in a forest filled with birds and squirrels or on a busy street in the middle of a large city, you join a community of living things in a specific physical environment. An ecosystem can be as big as our planet, with all its varied creatures (the biosphere), or as small as a pond, with particular species of frogs, fish, ducks, and plants. Soil, water, altitude, temperature, the amount of precipitation (rain or snow), as well as animal and plant life, define an ecosystem.

In this book you'll get to explore a dozen large ecosystems. There are a great many more in our world, but I chose these twelve because they represent some of the most fascinating areas on Earth, sheltering an amazing variety of creatures. Because animals in the Arctic and the Antarctic differ—polar bears in the north and penguins in the south— I decided to show both polar regions. The savanna ecosystem belongs to a larger category—the grasslands. Because each is home to a very different group of animals, I wanted to show an example of both.

Get ready to embark on twelve Earth adventures, solving the mazes with your finger as you go. Using trails, roads, or waterways, take the shortest path to the goal. Along the way, keep an eye out for some of the creatures that live in these ecosystems—there are more than 350 of them here for you to discover!

TROPICAL RAINFOREST

You're a biologist checking on the monkeys—find your way from the pier to the beach (and watch out for the jaguars!).

Find 2 roseate spoonbills, 3 macaws, a harpy eagle, a sloth, an armadillo, 2 jaguars, 4 monkeys, an anteater, a toucan, an emerald tree boa, and a caiman.

DESERT

Camels can go without water for weeks, but you're a nature photographer on this trek and you want to get to the oasis!

Find 5 camels, a fennec fox, a scorpion, a desert horned viper, a herd of 6 addax, a desert hedgehog, a cape hare, a desert eagle owl, and a slender mongoose.

CORAL REEF

Don't touch any of the fragile coral! But you and your buddy need to swim along the sandy ocean floor to get back to the beach.

Find 2 parrotfish, a reef shark, 2 stingrays, a spotted lionfish, a trumpet fish, a spotted moray eel, a seahorse, a grouper, 9 angelfish, 3 starfish, an octopus, and 2 butterfly fish.

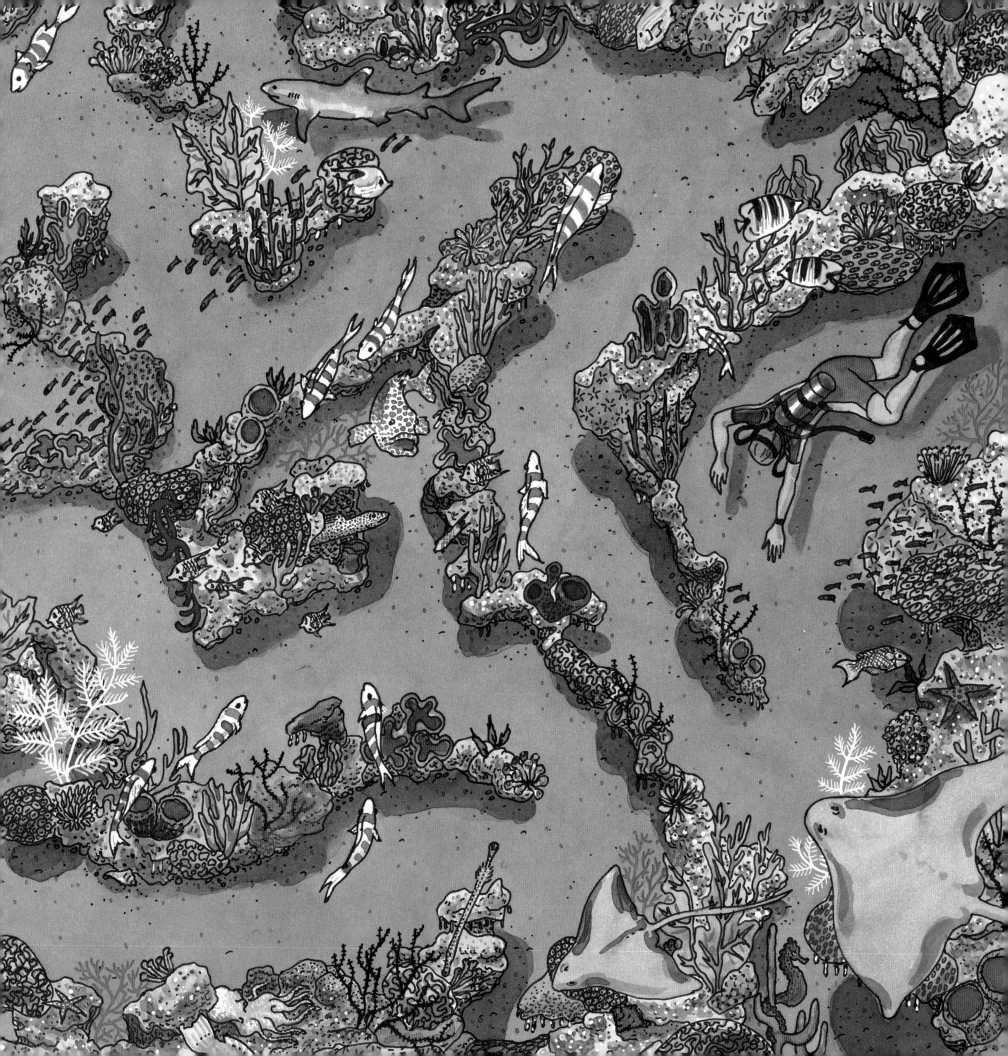

ALPINE HIGH MOUNTAIN

You're a scientist hiking from Base Camp to Upper Camp . . . will you catch a glimpse of the rare snow leopard?

Find a golden eagle, 5 yaks, a marmot, a wolf, a herd of blue sheep, and a snow leopard.

ARCTIC POLAR

Polar bears are good swimmers, but this mother bear and her three cubs need to find their way back to their snow den while staying on the ice floes.

Find 3 walruses, an arctic fox, a beluga whale, 3 puffins, 2 arctic terns, and a seal colony.

WETLANDS

You're a naturalist observing the alligator habitat and the wading birds. Don't scare them—paddle very quietly back to the pier.

Find an osprey, a purple gallinule, 3 roseate spoonbills, 7 wood ducks, a brown pelican, a great blue heron, a white ibis, an American bittern, a snowy egret, an oystercatcher, 3 alligators, an otter, a turtle, and a water moccasin.

TUNDRA

The reindeer and her fawn are foraging for food—they need to find their way to the big lakeshore where there is more foliage. But the tiny lemming just wants to go home to his burrow.

Find a spotted sandpiper, a weasel, 2 arctic swans, 2 flocks of migrating geese, a snowshoe hare, an arctic fox, and a snowy owl.

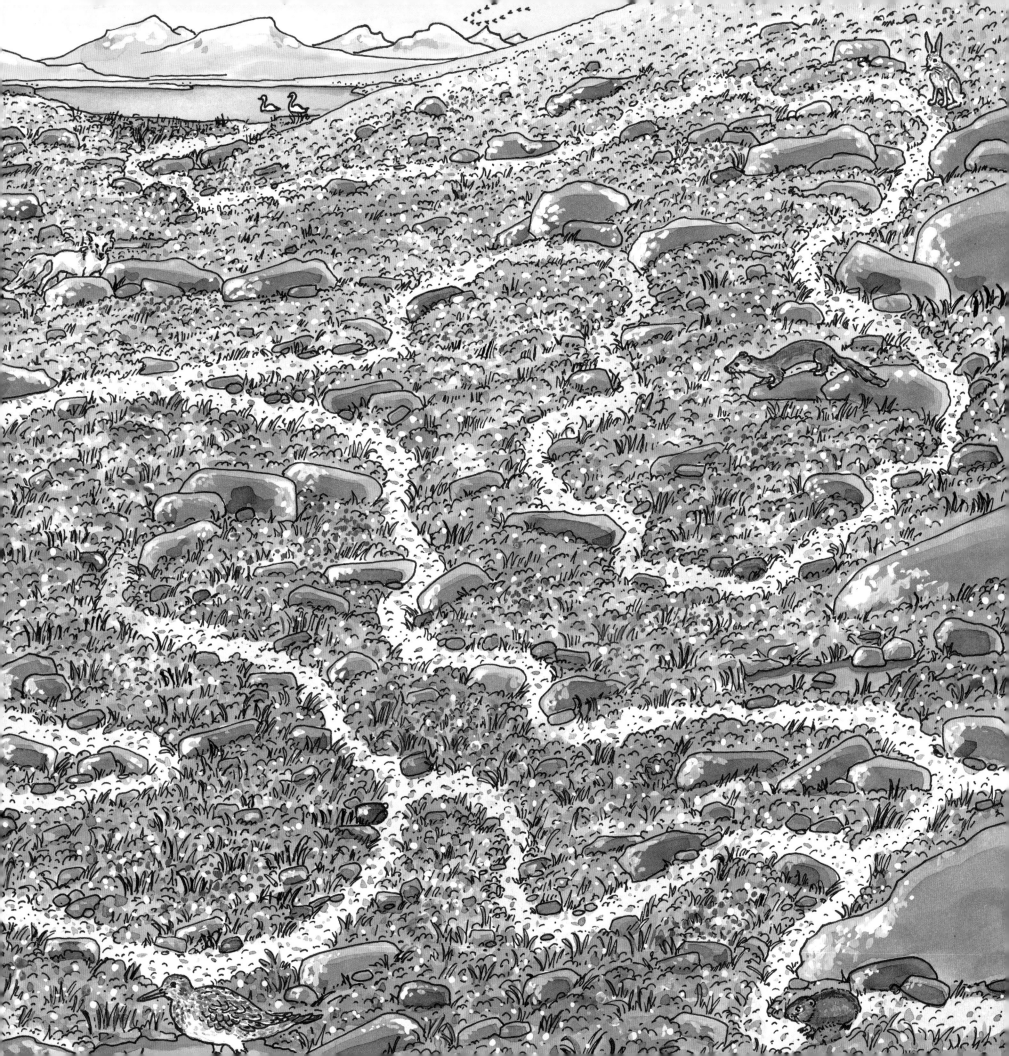

GRASSLANDS

You're a cowboy and have been up since dawn, but you still need to measure the creek water level and check on the cattle herd before you can head back home to ranch headquarters.

Find a coyote, a monarch butterfly, 3 buffaloes, a prairie dog, a raccoon, a skunk, a rattlesnake, a roadrunner, a vulture, a tarantula, 3 grouse, a jackrabbit, and a red-tailed hawk.

ANTARCTIC POLAR

Help the father penguin by the shore cliff on the left find his way back to the nest, where his two baby penguins are all alone and waiting for him.

Find 8 Weddell seals, a leopard seal, a sperm whale, and 2 snowy petrels.

SAVANNA

Guide the lost baby elephant back to his herd. His mom and aunts are anxious to have him safely home!

Find 5 lions, a herd of zebras, 2 leopards, 12 ostriches, 2 rhinos, 4 hippos, 14 giraffes, a crocodile, 7 antelopes, a herd of Cape buffalo, and some termite hills.

CONIFER FOREST

This last beaver on the hill needs to get to work—he should grab a branch, start swimming, and do his part to help build the dam!

Find a shrew, 7 deer, a flock of Canada geese, an owl, a spotted woodpecker, a red fox, a brown bear, a hare, and a moose.

TEMPERATE FOREST

Pick up trash along the beach and put it in the recycling containers, check on the horses, gather fresh vegetables from the garden and drop them off at the dining hall, and then go to the campfire to roast marshmallows . . . you're as busy as the other creatures in this ecosystem!

Find a red-headed woodpecker, 2 mallard ducks, an owl, a bear, 4 deer, a raccoon, 4 horses, a skunk, a red fox, a gray squirrel, and a red-tailed hawk.

TROPICAL RAINFOREST

A rainforest may get between 80 and 400 inches of rain in a year!

Take a walk in a tropical rainforest, and you'll find a noisy, highly colorful world. Toucans, frogs, and butterflies show off bright colors and rich patterns. Howler monkeys, parrots, and many other creatures fill the air with their loud chatter. Snakes coil around branches, monkeys use their tails to swing from tree to tree, and there are busy insects everywhere you look.

Each rainforest has its own special animals. So, for instance, only in an African rainforest will you find gorillas, hippos, and elephants living together.

Did you know that more than half of the world's plant and animal species live in tropical rainforests? Covering about 6% of Earth's land surface, they offer a wider variety of living creatures than any other ecosystem.

The maze here is based on a South American tropical rainforest. Other tropical rainforests can also be found in Africa, Central America, Southeast Asia, the South Pacific, and Australia. Since many of these regions are found near the equator, they are warm and wet year round and get about the same amount of daylight throughout the year.

Tropical rainforests have been called "Earth's lungs," as well as the "world's largest pharmacy." Sadly, many rainforests were destroyed in the 20th century, mostly because of excessive logging, but people all over the world are now working hard to preserve those that still remain.

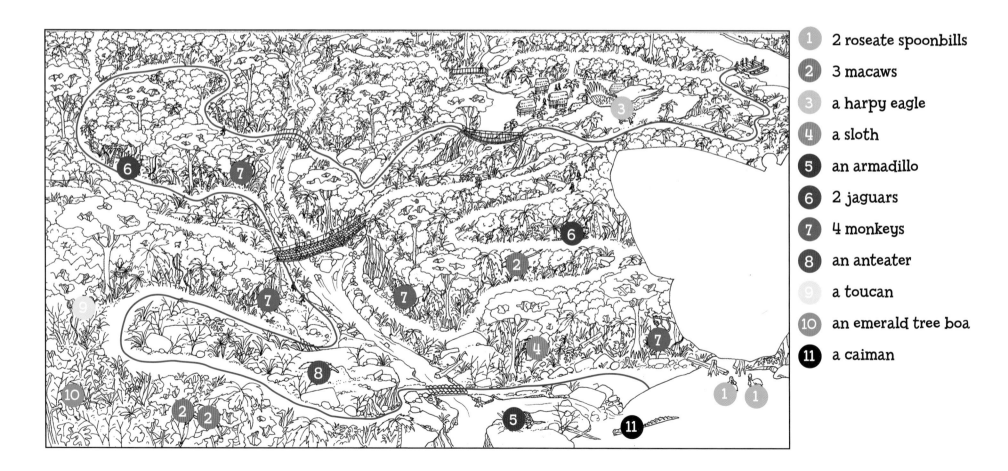

1 2 roseate spoonbills
2 3 macaws
3 a harpy eagle
4 a sloth
5 an armadillo
6 2 jaguars
7 4 monkeys
8 an anteater
9 a toucan
10 an emerald tree boa
11 a caiman

ANSWER KEY

DESERT

You almost missed seeing it—a slithering, winding snake, almost as long as you are tall. But lots of animals in the desert are sand-colored and blend into the landscape. This one certainly did!

There are few large mammals in the desert, because they can't store much water or withstand the heat, and there is little shelter—just sand, rocks, small shrubs, and a few trees. Deserts can get very hot during the day, but quite cold at night. Most animals in the desert are reptiles, birds, or small burrowing rodents. Deserts often appear to be empty but are actually full of life. Many animals are nocturnal, so they won't come out until after dark, when it cools down.

There are four major kinds of deserts. Arid deserts, which are hot and dry, are found in low altitudes in the Americas, Australia, and Africa. This maze is modeled on the Sahara desert. Semi-arid deserts are not as hot and dry, and are located in North America, Russia, Europe, and Asia. In these deserts, much of the vegetation has spines or glossy leaves to conserve water and reflect the blazing sun. Located in Chile, the Atacama, which is the driest place on Earth, is an example of a coastal desert. Here, very few plants and animals can survive. Finally, there are cold deserts, in Greenland, near the polar regions, and in North America. They have cold winters with snow, and short warm summers. Plants are widely scattered, but there can be a lot of sagebrush and some grasses. Living in some cold deserts are jackrabbits, deer (in the winter), and many burrowing animals, including rodents, foxes, and even burrowing coyotes!

One-fifth of the planet is desert and extremely dry, with scarcely any rain at all.

1 5 camels
2 a fennec fox
3 a scorpion
4 a desert horned viper
5 a herd of 6 addax
6 a desert hedgehog
7 a cape hare
8 a desert eagle owl
9 a slender mongoose

ANSWER KEY

CORAL REEF

The Great Barrier Reef in Australia is the largest reef system on Earth. It's half the size of Texas, and it has 629 species of seaweed!

You've passed the diving course, and have traveled to this South Pacific atoll. Now, in the shallow sunlit ocean waters, you see, for the first time, a tiny seahorse and a colorful parrotfish. Silently, a reef shark passes slowly by. It is more magical, more alive, than you ever imagined.

Coral reefs are created in shallow warm water in tropical oceans around the Equator. They are found along coastlines, near volcanic islands, and rise to or near the surface in the form of a barrier reef, fringing reef, or atoll (an island made of coral).

A coral reef is slowly formed by the skeletons of many thousands of polyps, tiny simple creatures related to jellyfish and anemones. Each new generation builds on top of the skeletons of the old ones. Colonies of coral make elaborate, brightly-colored structures, with fun names like "brain" corals, "antler," "elephant ear," and "fan" corals.

Coral reefs are full of life. Although they cover less than 1% of Earth's surface, they are home to more than a quarter of all marine fish species, as well as sea stars, octopi, sea urchins, and other fascinating creatures. Because coral reefs have such rich diversity of life, they are sometimes called the "rainforests of the ocean." These are some of the oldest, but most fragile, ecosystems on Earth. With just a slight rise in the water temperature, usually constant throughout the year, the coral can become white, an event known as bleaching.

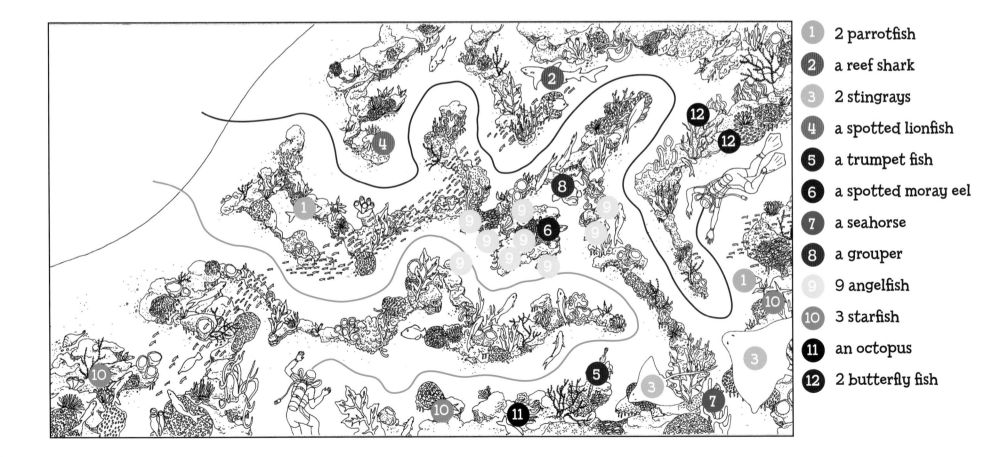

1. 2 parrotfish
2. a reef shark
3. 2 stingrays
4. a spotted lionfish
5. a trumpet fish
6. a spotted moray eel
7. a seahorse
8. a grouper
9. 9 angelfish
10. 3 starfish
11. an octopus
12. 2 butterfly fish

ANSWER KEY

ALPINE HIGH MOUNTAIN

Your hiking boots crunch over the frozen ground—you've only been walking a little while, but already you are short of breath. A marmot whistles nearby, and a golden eagle soars high above your head. You hear the distant roar of a waterfall. . . .

High mountain alpine ecosystems are usually above the tree line, approximately 10,000 feet above sea level, where no big trees can grow. The soil is poor, sandy, and rocky, and most of the plants (small shrubs, some grasses, lichen, moss, and tiny mountain flowers) are low to the ground. The few animals that live in this cold, dry, and windy environment have heavy fur to keep them warm. Winter is long with lots of snow, and summer is short and cool.

The mountain landscape is rocky, with cliffs and boulders, and sometimes lakes, streams, and waterfalls. Humans rarely live above the tree line—not only is the climate harsh, offering no sustenance, but there is less oxygen available as the altitude increases. This maze is based on the Himalayas in Asia, a mountain chain with some of the world's highest peaks, but alpine ecosystems can be found on all seven continents—even Antarctica.

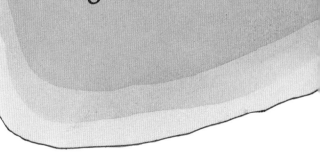

Temperatures can change from warm to below freezing in the same day!

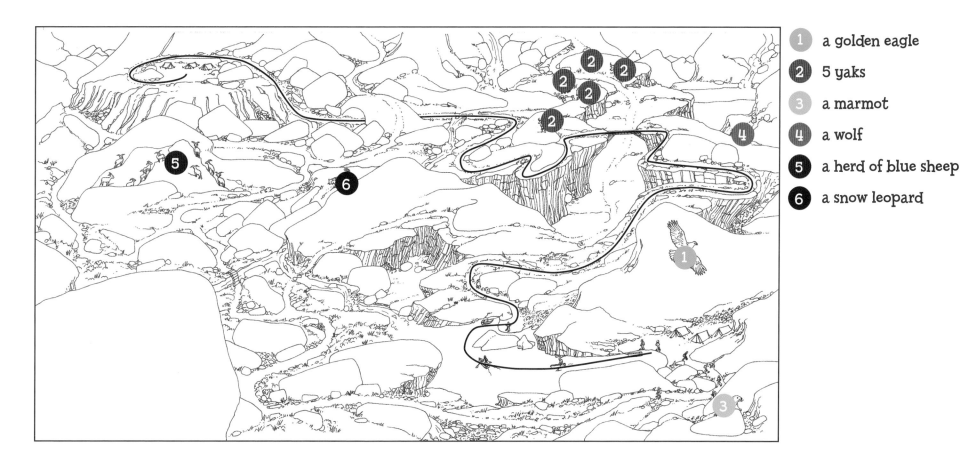

1. a golden eagle
2. 5 yaks
3. a marmot
4. a wolf
5. a herd of blue sheep
6. a snow leopard

ANSWER KEY

ARCTIC POLAR

In the Arctic, ice covers approximately 5.5 million square miles, but shrinks to about half that amount in the summer.

Imagine yourself at the North Pole. You'd be in the middle of a cold, quiet, white world. There's ice everywhere—no trees, no plants, no green.

But there are some animals hardy enough to live in this harsh environment. Walruses and seals have thick layers of blubber to insulate them from the cold water, ice, and winds. Some animals, like the polar bear and arctic fox, are white or light-colored to blend in with the landscape. Certain fish even have a special protein in their blood that acts like antifreeze, so they can survive in the icy waters. Animals feed on a variety of marine life—zooplankton, crustaceans, mollusks, worms, and fish. And many birds make the Arctic their summer home.

The polar regions—the North and South Poles—are the coldest places on Earth. Even more dramatic are changes in light from one season to the other. In the summer, the sun never sets—it shines 24 hours a day. But during the winter months, it stays dark all day and night.

The North Pole is in the middle of the ice-covered Arctic Ocean, surrounded by the northernmost part of North America, Greenland, Europe, and Siberia. Six- to eight-foot ice floes float on the water at the North Pole. In recent years, polar ice has melted at an accelerated rate. These regions are fragile and particularly vulnerable to pollution, over-fishing, and climate changes.

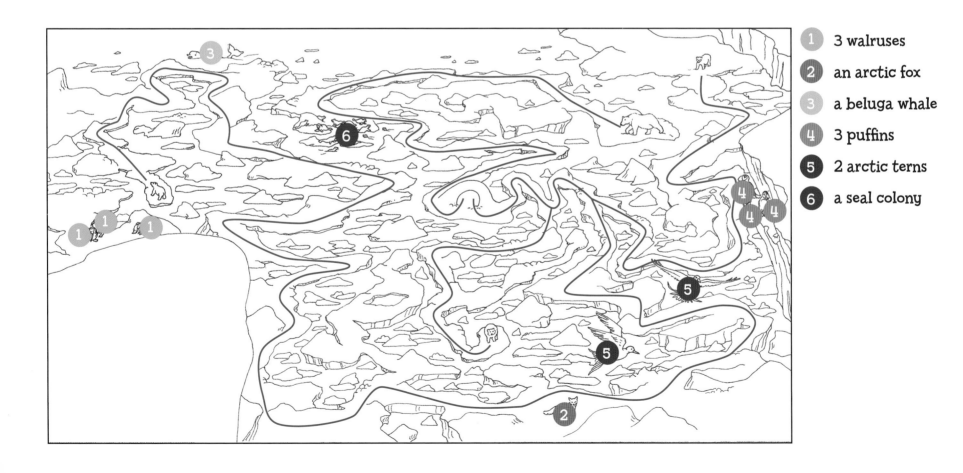

1 3 walruses

2 an arctic fox

3 a beluga whale

4 3 puffins

5 2 arctic terns

6 a seal colony

ANSWER KEY

WETLANDS

Luminous green water, golden reeds, and, here and there, an alligator sunning itself on a half-submerged log—you're in the Florida Everglades, one of the largest wetlands in the world.

Up to one-half of North American bird species nest, feed, or rest on their migration routes in wetlands. It is also a home or a spawning place for many fish, and a habitat for reptiles and small mammals.

Some wetlands are temporary and seasonal. Others are always under water. The term "wetlands" includes swamps, marshes, and bogs. In a swamp, which is actually a slow-moving stream, you'll usually find trees and shrubs. A marsh has reeds, grasses, rushes, and cattails and is usually treeless and open. Marshes can be shallow or deep. In deeper marshes, pondweeds and water lilies float on the water.

Salt marshes, often rich with plant and animal life, usually fluctuate with the tide and are found along coasts near river mouths, around protected lagoons, and on broad coastal plains. A bog is wet and spongy from precipitation—there's usually no direct in or out flow of water. In some bogs, the vegetation forms a floating mat almost like a water bed that you can jump up and down on (but wear a hat in case you fall through, so people can find you)!

Sadly, many wetlands have disappeared in the last 100 years, and many are threatened by pollution, development, and drought. Wetlands serve an important function, nourishing wildlife and fish. They also filter and cleanse water. Much like a sponge, they absorb excess water during storms and prevent flooding.

The largest reptile in the USA, the alligator, lives in the Everglades. The longest ever found was over 19 feet long!

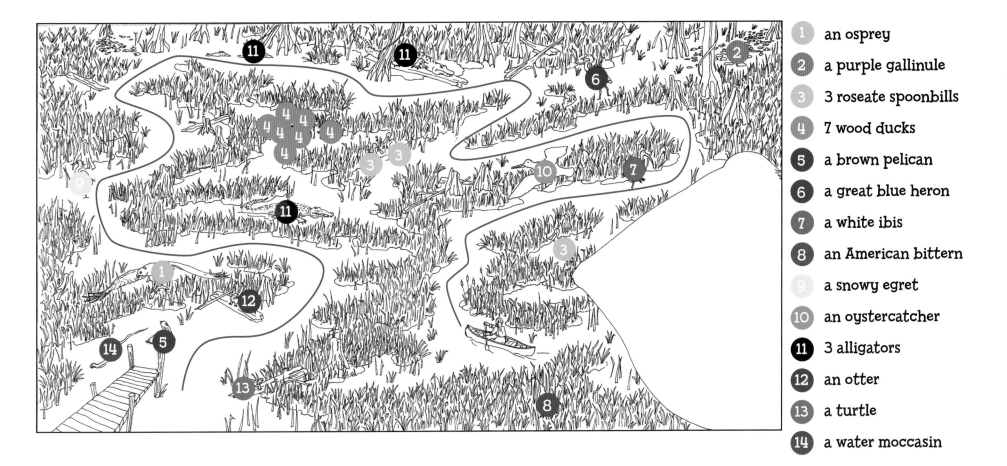

1. an osprey
2. a purple gallinule
3. 3 roseate spoonbills
4. 7 wood ducks
5. a brown pelican
6. a great blue heron
7. a white ibis
8. an American bittern
9. a snowy egret
10. an oystercatcher
11. 3 alligators
12. an otter
13. a turtle
14. a water moccasin

ANSWER KEY

TUNDRA

For at least nine months a year, the temperature is well below freezing (-30° F or -34° C).

The word "tundra" comes from the Finnish word <u>tunturia</u>, which means a barren treeless land. You may think you've landed on a frozen prairie, with lots of pebbles and rocks, but don't confuse it with a prairie in the western USA!

This is a cold, barren place, with winds blowing up to 60 miles per hour. Sometimes, during the short summer, you may see bogs or ponds, but just below the surface there's a layer of permanently frozen subsoil, from 10 inches to hundreds of feet deep, called permafrost. Because of this layer, trees with long roots can't grow here. However, small shrubs, lichen, mosses, grasses, and tiny flowers grow, but at a very slow rate. And the soil is so fragile that a tire track or a footprint can leave permanent scars, preventing plant re-growth for years. This maze is based upon a tundra in Russia—most tundras are found in high latitudes in the Northern Hemisphere.

The animals that live there have adapted to this harsh environment. Many have heavy fur and layers of fat, and some hibernate during the dark, cold winter months. During the brief summer, when the top of the permafrost thaws, millions of insects breed, attracting migrating birds. There are very few reptiles or amphibians because of the severe cold.

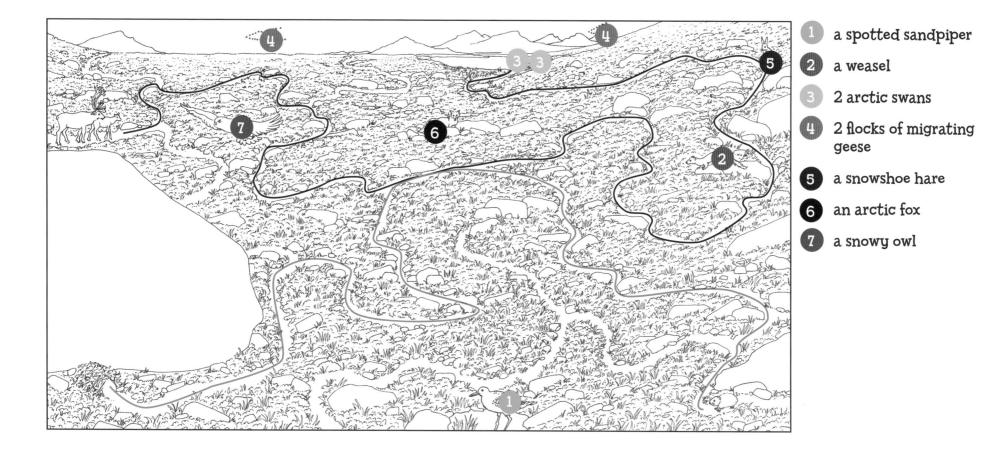

1 a spotted sandpiper
2 a weasel
3 2 arctic swans
4 2 flocks of migrating geese
5 a snowshoe hare
6 an arctic fox
7 a snowy owl

ANSWER KEY

GRASSLANDS

If you were a cowboy right now in the American West, you'd probably work in a typical grassland—usually flat, with rich, fertile soil, and many different kinds of grasses. It's good for grazing animals, like cattle, horses, and sheep, but also has lots of wildlife, from deer and wolves to snakes and butterflies, and many birds.

Grasslands get little rain except in late spring and early summer. With the extra precipitation, hundreds of wildflowers of all colors blossom, sometimes covering the land like a multi-colored quilt. There are some large shrubs, and a few trees (like oaks, willows, and cottonwoods) that grow in the river valleys.

The western grassland shown in this maze can also be called a prairie. Drier grasslands with shorter grasses are called steppes—they can be found in Russia, parts of Europe, and the Americas. Savannas, which are also featured in this book, are another type of grassland.

It can get very hot in the summer, often over 100° F (38° C), and extremely cold in the winter, with temperatures as low as -40° F (-40° C).

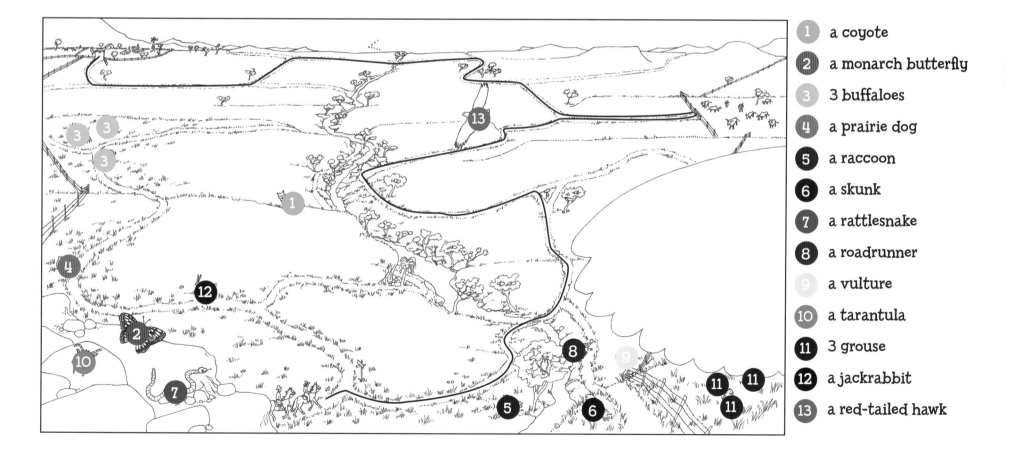

1. a coyote
2. a monarch butterfly
3. 3 buffaloes
4. a prairie dog
5. a raccoon
6. a skunk
7. a rattlesnake
8. a roadrunner
9. a vulture
10. a tarantula
11. 3 grouse
12. a jackrabbit
13. a red-tailed hawk

ANSWER KEY

ANTARCTIC POLAR

Antarctica has the lowest ever temperature recorded on Earth (-129.28° F or -89.6° C)!

It's summer. You're standing on a rocky coast, surrounded by high ice-covered peaks. Within sight are hundreds of black and white Adelie penguins, huddled over their nests made of small stones. Suddenly in the clear cold air you hear a sharp crack, followed by a distant roar. It's a glacier "calving"—ice breaking loose and falling into the sea. You're at the bottom of the world—"The White Continent"—Antarctica.

Ninety-eight percent of Antarctica, the land that sits on top of the South Pole, is covered in ice. It is the coldest place on earth—colder than the Arctic because most of it is well above sea level and temperature drops with elevation. Antarctica has 90% of the world's ice—in some areas the ice is over a mile thick—and is the windiest place on earth. In 2000, the biggest iceberg ever recorded broke free from the Ross Ice Shelf in Antarctica. It was 183 miles long, 25 miles wide—about the size of Connecticut—and rose 120 feet. And that was just a small portion of it since 90% of this humongous chunk of ice was below water level!

Although few animals can survive in such a cold climate, there are several kinds of seals and whales that live there. Birds include albatross, petrels, doves, cormorants, gulls, terns, and pintails. In the Arctic there are no penguins, but here you'll find them by the millions—17 different species—among them Adelie, macaroni, chinstrap, emperor, gentoo, and Humboldt.

1. 8 Weddell seals
2. a leopard seal
3. a sperm whale
4. 2 snowy petrels

ANSWER KEY

SAVANNA

You're on a safari! At night in the hut you hear the roar of a hungry lion; in the jeep ride in the morning a huge herd of zebras thunders by....

There are plenty of animals from African savannas seen in this maze—from long-necked giraffes to hippos, snakes, worms, beetles, and termites. Sometimes, when elephants destroy trees by eating the leaves, breaking the branches, and stripping off the bark, forest areas can be turned into savannas.

Savannas are a type of grassland, and cover almost half of the land in Africa. They are also found in warm or hot areas of India, South America, and Australia (which has some unique animals, like kangaroos). Savannas alternate between rainy and dry seasons. Heavy monsoon rains, usually 15 to 25 inches, begin in late spring. In the dry season an average of only about 4 inches of rain falls, and thunderstorms often cause fires. This is not necessarily a bad thing.

Most animals will escape, and the grass roots remain unharmed. Then, as soon as it rains, the grass quickly recuperates, bringing new life to the savanna.

Plant life is adapted to the hot and dry climate. Some plants lie dormant (alive but not growing) during the drought, and some tree trunks are able to store water for a long time. Trees have long roots in order to extract water from deep below ground, and small, waxy, and thorny leaves, so that less moisture is lost through evaporation.

More than 40 different species of hoofed mammals live on the savannas of Africa!

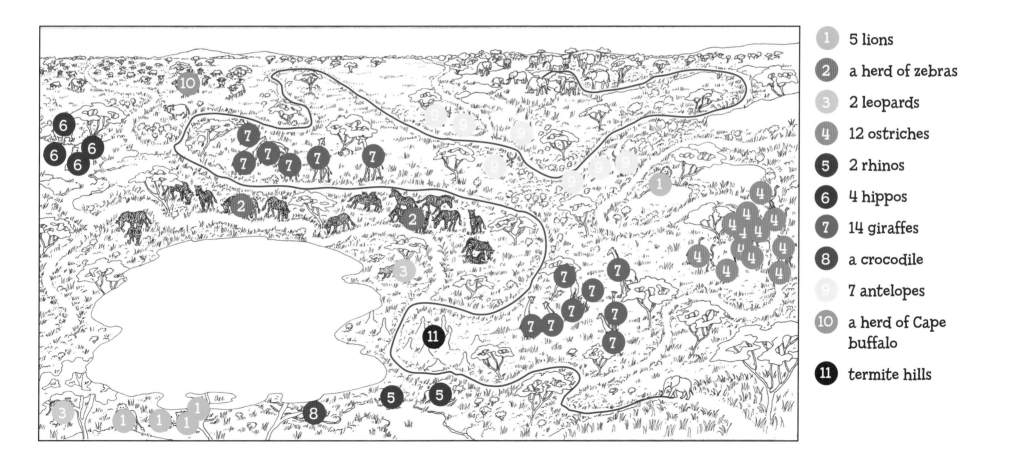

1 5 lions
2 a herd of zebras
3 2 leopards
4 12 ostriches
5 2 rhinos
6 4 hippos
7 14 giraffes
8 a crocodile
9 7 antelopes
10 a herd of Cape buffalo
11 termite hills

ANSWER KEY

CONIFER FOREST

Coniferous forests are sometimes called taiga or boreal forests.

Be careful! A brown bear is not to be trifled with, and here it is one of the animals you may run into, along with elk, moose, and deer.

Conifer forests have dense evergreen trees, like pines, firs, or spruces. These forests are found only in the Northern Hemisphere—North America, Russia, Asia, and northern Europe (like this maze set in Scandinavia). They are dotted with lakes, bogs, and marshes, and have a narrower variety of plants and animals than deciduous or rainforests. Because of the climate—short, moist, relatively warm summers and long, dry, cold winters—plant life in the conifer forest is sturdy. And with a dense canopy of evergreens shutting out light, there isn't much forest floor vegetation.

Most conifer forest creatures are well adapted to the cold climate. The snowshoe hare has large paws for running easily over the snow, and in the winter, to blend in with the snow, his fur changes its color to white. Some animals burrow beneath the snow and forage for their food in tunnels along the forest floor. Others, like bears, hibernate in the winter, and many, like elk, moose, and birds, migrate to warmer regions. Very few cold-blooded amphibians and reptiles live among the conifers. During the brief summer, the forest fills up with millions of insects, providing a plentiful food supply for birds.

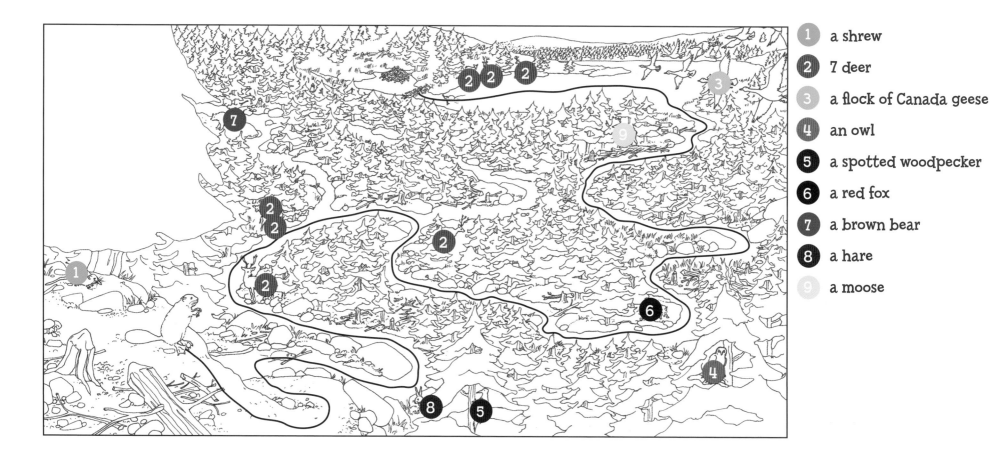

1. a shrew
2. 7 deer
3. a flock of Canada geese
4. an owl
5. a spotted woodpecker
6. a red fox
7. a brown bear
8. a hare
9. a moose

ANSWER KEY

TEMPERATE FOREST

A raccoon sneaks around the back of your tent looking for food, a woodpecker taps loudly, and you see a glimpse of a white-tailed deer through the trees....

You are part of an ecosystem no matter where you are. An ecosystem can be as small as a household or a school, and as large as a city, a state, or a country. The Earth itself is one huge human ecosystem, with people inhabiting most of its surface. The campground shown here is an ecosystem of people and animals living together in the same environment.

This maze also shows a temperate deciduous forest ecosystem. Deciduous trees, unlike evergreens, are trees that shed their leaves for part of every year. Come fall, the foliage turns into a symphony of brilliant colors—reds, oranges, and yellows. The trees remain bare through the winter until they grow tender new green leaves each spring. Some of the more common deciduous trees include ash, beech, birch, maple, poplar, hickory, locust, chestnut, linden, oak, and cottonwood. Soil is rich and fertile with organic decay. Although it has fewer species than a rainforest, a deciduous forest is full of animals—mammals (some hibernate or burrow in the winter), reptiles, insects, and many birds.

Forests (conifer, rainforest, and deciduous) cover one-third of the Earth's land. Although usually located in the tropics, rainforests also grow in temperate regions. Temperate deciduous forests are found in eastern North America, northeastern Asia, and Europe. They have four seasons—spring, summer, autumn, and winter. This maze, which also shows a human ecosystem, depicts a deciduous forest in North America in early autumn.

Some oak trees can live for 600 years!

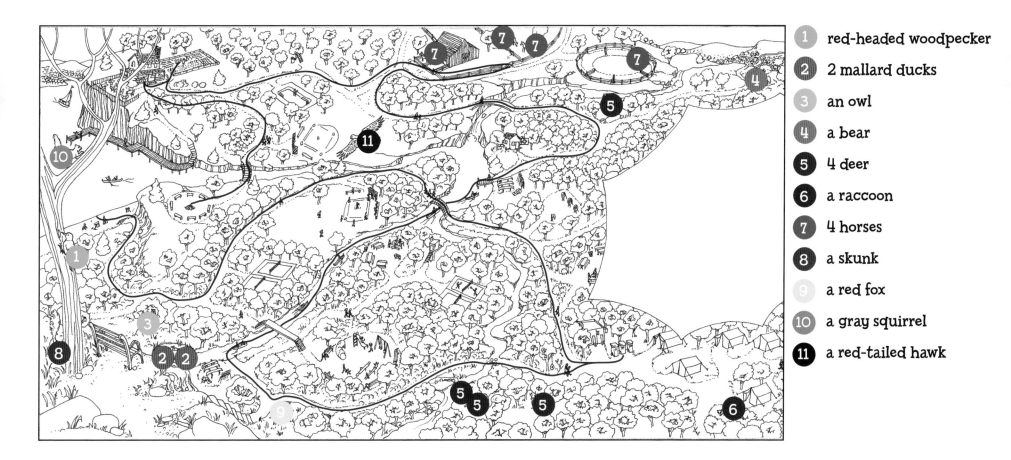

1	red-headed woodpecker
2	2 mallard ducks
3	an owl
4	a bear
5	4 deer
6	a raccoon
7	4 horses
8	a skunk
9	a red fox
10	a gray squirrel
11	a red-tailed hawk

ANSWER KEY

Dear Reader,

Researching this book on ecosystems was a lot of fun! In the year I worked on it, I tramped through rainforests in the Marquesas Islands, watched polar bears on Svalbard high above the Arctic Circle, glimpsed reef sharks in Tahiti, and picked mushrooms in a Swedish conifer forest.

In the United States, I've snorkeled through coral reefs off Hawaii, climbed into alpine territory on the highest mountain in the lower 48 states, traveled through five North American deserts, and camped out in the temperate forests of Maine and West Virginia. I grew up in the wetlands of the Chesapeake Bay, and have paddled around Mississippi Delta marshes.

Think about where you live and where you have traveled—make a list. I predict that you have been to more of the ecosystems shown in this book than you might imagine. And if not . . . you have a lot to look forward to!

Roxie Munro

Want to know more about earth science and ecosystems? Check out these resources:

http://www.mbgnet.net/
Missouri Botanical Garden

http://www.ucmp.berkeley.edu/exhibits/biomes/index.php
University of California Museum of Paleontology

http://earthobservatory.nasa.gov/Experiments/Biome/index.php
National Aeronautics and Space Administration

http://kids.nceas.ucsb.edu/biomes/index.html
National Center for Ecological Analysis and Synthesis

http://www.epa.gov/teachers/ecosystems.htm
Environmental Protection Agency

http://www.panda.org/about_our_earth/ecoregions/ecoregion_list/
World Wildlife Fund

Bishop, Nic. *Forest Explorer: A Life-Sized Field Guide.*
New York: Scholastic, Inc., 2004.

David, Laurie and Cambria Gordon. *The Down-to-Earth Guide to Global Warming.* New York: Orchard Books, 2007.

Pfeffer, Wendy. *Life in a Coral Reef.*
New York: Collins, 2009.

Strauss, Rochelle. *Tree of Life: The Incredible Biodiversity of Life on Earth.* A & C Black Publishers Ltd., 2005.

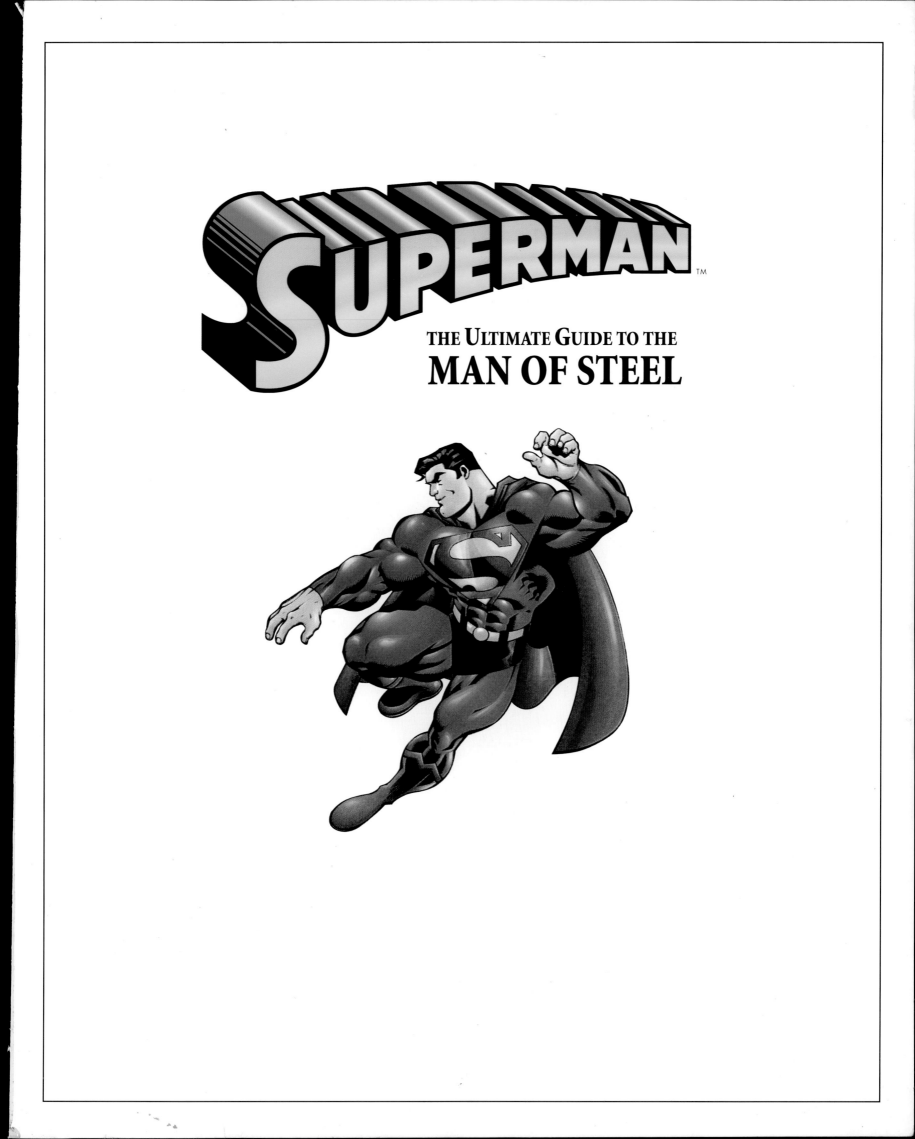

Dorling **DK** Kindersley

LONDON, NEW YORK, MUNICH,
MELBOURNE, and DELHI

Senior Editor Alastair Dougall
Senior Designer Robert Perry
Publishing Manager Cynthia O'Neill
Art Director Cathy Tincknell
Production Nicola Torode
DTP Designer Jill Bunyan

02 03 04 05 10 9 8 7 6 5 4 3 2

Published in the United States by
DK Publishing Inc., 375 Hudson Street, New York, NY 10014, USA.

Library of Congress Cataloging-in-Publication Data

Beatty, Scott, 1969-
Superman : the ultimate guide to the Man of Steel / by Scott Beatty.--
1st America ed.
p. cm.
ISBN 0-7894-8853-1
1. Superman (Comic strip)--Juvenile literature. I. Title.
PN6728.S9 B43 2002
741.5'973--dc21
2002019494

Color reproduction by Media Development and Printing Ltd., UK
Printed and bound in Spain by Mondadori.

Visit DC Comics online at www.dccomics.com or at keyword DC Comics on America Online.

see our complete product line at
www.dk.com